chrysalis

under

fire

by douglas powell/roscoe burnems

"I am going to be black and dangerous and that is never going to change."

~Jacob Mayberry (Black Chakra)

table of contents

when they say

it's because he was a criminal.

        do not crime

because she was being aggressive.

        do not aggress

because they were wearing a hood.

        do not be hooded

because he was big.

        do not be big

when you have nothing but your body.

        do not body

        do not move

        do not breathe

or they will take it

gun down your character

and leave it a carcass

to rot in the streets

your body is only the beginning

it is truth in your throat that will hang

amongst the wall of spectacles before you

a gallery of

                misconstrued

                misunderstood

                misappropriated

when you say it's because you are black

you will hear

do not be you

do not be human

do not be oppressed in the company of your
oppressors

what they are saying is

do not be high enough to sit with them

but do not be low enough to have excuses

be middle of the road

side of the road

roadkill

tar

black shadow

hiding black fist

     fist is aggressive

     do not aggress

75 percent of accused criminals are black

     do not crime

and even when you don't

be prepared to   not do

whatever they make you

       next.

rerun

while watching the movie *warm bodies*,
hands-down one of the most ridiculously corny
zombie flicks ever made, i do what i normally do
during horrible films... drift off while pondering the
complexities of life. most unfortunate while a
poorly written "love story" about the undead
is plucking at my rem sleep. what begins as
questions about *how the fuck zombies even get out
of coffins anyway*, turns into, how we've all lost
someone we never expect to say goodbye to so
soon. how tears have petitioned the soil to unhand
loved ones and sprout from the earth.

it sounds entertaining, heartwarming, but what if
that shit really happened?!

people who've passed, turned undead, came back at
our request.
climbed a wretched 6 feet to the surface to walk
among us. mass chaos! brain eating monsters!
right?! but we've seen this before. media attempt at
creating a threat that isn't real. what if zombies care
nothing about apocalypse, but more about
assimilation, representation. what if zombies want
rights, respect, and votes.

vote the first zombie president into office,
zombie marriage legalization,
adoption.

that's scarier than any terror threat.

america chooses who gets to be human.

watch hollywood show us how to destroy a people:
news spins culture into villain. police turn rebellious
bodies into the walking dead. we watch cnn call it
an invasion when the zombies call it a protest. state
senator frankenstein's a narrative about denying
rights somehow gives america more freedom.
growling decay is what's portrayed on every hd
screen.

maybe they never show zombies talking because
america doesn't like what they have to say

blood-filled veins will say the word "undead" like a
slur like it's not a synonym for alive; say it the way
they say "terrorists", or "thug" or "gay". people will
claim their heartbeat makes them superior, condemn
zombies with hellish rhetoric. use religion to
explain them, confine, disguise them. make-up sales
will spike. grey peeling bodies will paint themselves
a rosy tan to fearfully protect the living's social

conditioning.

it will do what america does...
vilify.
scrutinize.
minimize their love.
mummify their culture.
crater them into prejudice.
cast an interrogating eye into their beds
'til they can't sleep.
all because some humans don't understand
that all things -living or dead- just want rest and
peace.

ars poetica slam: black-ass poems

we get it! shit is fucked up!
we all tired! all lives are tired!
tired!   of black-ass poems!
every poetry slam is full of angry black-ass poets!

we gotta talk about some different shit!

like sports!
football!
woo! go... team?!
without mentioning
        runaway field niggas
        to niggas running on a field
        buying freedom from free labor
        giving up free agency to highest bidder on
auction blocks
        balling out at a combine.
scanning biceps and thighs for the
biggest and strongest buck
plays for the redskins or the buc's
for the big bucks
but cant stand up   or take a knee

kaep

dammit i'm talking about black shit again!
let's try something else.

music!
not rap music (too easy).
country music!
it can't get more non-black than that!
johnny cash! bob dylan!

both of which attribute their start to odetta.
odetta, black-woman-folk-singer who made the
genre popular.
odetta, persecuted for anti-american folk songs
during the civil rights movement.
[meanwhile] bob dylan gets **praised** for
anti-american folk songs during the civil rights
movement.
guess guitar strings sound different when it's cotton
in your jeans and not under your nails.
now country music is all
10 gallon hats,
rodeos,
cowboy boots.
which is actually very black
since in Texas
1 in 4 cowboys were african-american
(google it).

it's hard trying to just write a "regular poem"
when i see so much of my skin in everything.

for me being a dad is a black poem:
my kids are 28 times more likely to be shot 28 times
by the time they turn 28.

for me, being a teacher is a black poem:
my student's neighborhoods are robert frost cliches
drenched in systemic oppression.
their streets look like roads less travelled
less funded
more patrolled
my students are all little beautiful black-ass poems!
you want all the black poets to stop
writing all the angry black poems...
stop giving us so much material.

white poets get the luxury to write about *fun shit*!
haikus about star wars and shit!
starbucks and shit!

haiku:
you know, i prefer
my jedis same way i pre-
fer my coffee... black!

children of the drum

"white folks hear the blues come out, but they don't know how it got there." -ma rainey

a timeline of music

went from drum call to call for freedom
from plucking on banjos to bondage on a ship
from djembes to django

then crash
on the soil of tobacco cotton sharecroppin
fingers
coarse as their hair
coarse as the lashes on their back
coarse as their pain.

harmonized   in the key of trauma
traumatized to the harm of being a minor
looking for the freedom   notes
slave song rebellion anthem
mapping north like a union soldiers bugle

same fingers
plucking strings   of blues
and folk guitars
same fingers

plucking the tear soaked rope from their necks

who but us could unhinge a noose
and turn into an instrument

go through hell, and make gospel
like fire shut up in the bones of a burning cross
baptize themselves in a colored fountain
who but negroes could fry a jim crow
and feed a nation revolution
to the symphony of the iron-hand-bigot called
america
the pop of gunshots and police batons like snare
snared justice   in the teeth of police dogs

who but colored folk could find the rhythm
in a riot
make jazz out of jail
make a motown out of a march
in formation til the
the soul need a breakbeat
we bass-boom and crack walls
crack glass ceilings
crack babies   born in a concrete existence
projects built like mausoleums
forced fed products of experimental
drugs gone viral
viruses gone viral

fame at the expense of an epidemic
[we] pump up the volume and the veins

who but blacks could use needles
to spin back the hands of time
and scratch
the surface of broken history
the one america tries to skip

who but descendants of slave
now only slave to the rhythm
could take generations of suffering
and make genres full of joy
and rising   sounds   like
black notes are the only reason music exist

how did it get there?!
we took the off-key we were given
remixed it into resilient medley.
while they try to silence the notes
hit the notes
dead the notes
it is said you can kill a revolutionary
but can't kill the revolution
when you are children of the drum
people can stop the hearts
but they can never stop the beat

metaphysics 101 for white privilege

if a tree falls in the forest and no one claims to hear,
did it make a sound?
what if the tree was rosewood?
what if it were a dark shade of brown?
would it matter? (or are you one of those "all trees
matter" type of people?)
what if the tree didn't fall? what if it were *chopped*
down?
what if the axe was targeting that tree?
what if that tree only made up 13 percent of the
woods but 60 percent of the caskets?
what if the tree had its branches stretched like first
day of spring?
tried to comply and still died.
is its death still a death?

is death, *death* when no one recognizes the life?

metaphysics is a broad philosophy.
[it] challenges what we think is real.
how things can be both seen and unseen at once.
like sound. like breath. like god. like death.
like people of color in america.

the nature of *being* is the perennial topic in

metaphysics.
and when discussing race
poses the question that only white people get to ask
themselves in this country:
"what does it mean to *be*?"

that is privilege;
the ability to question, decide, define.
create the standard and live in it without even
knowing it; the ability to *tell*.

people of color are often *told* to what to *be*:
be cargo, be commodity, be cash crop
be free   labor,
be free but this-water-fountain-free
be this side of the border
be terrorist, be under attack
be underrepresented
underfunded
undereducated but overwhelmed
be affirmative action,
(actually affirmative action statistically helps more
white women than any other demographic)
[so] be just enough to make the campus look
diverse
be voting when it's convenient
be voting when they need you
when they don't, be gerrymandered out of a voice

be
        quiet,
[because] if it doesn't make a sound,
then it doesn't exist.
this country is full of static and erasure
just because you didn't create the interference
doesn't mean you don't benefit from it

you cannot make the struggle in my skin a theory.
you cannot philosophy the death
of brown people in america.
we are not a hypothesis.
we are absolute.
an axiom.
an undeniable truth.
the plight for us isn't always trumps and rebel flags
sometimes it's the people
standing idly in the forest
        pretending
        not to hear us

        fall.

Lycanthropy: a black boy story

lycanthropy is the term describing the supernatural transformation of a person into a werewolf, like in movies and folktales.
it is also known as a form of madness involving the delusion of being an animal.

monday mornings,
jeremiah walks into my class growl ready.
foaming at the mouth with struggle.
his teeth have been snarling the entire weekend.

king of his den.
        only man in his house.

jeremiah is seven
        and already howls at a full moon.

in class is when the daylight hits.
you can tell it is warm and foreign.
the claws retracts, he walks erect.
he tries to smile,
plays with the other boys.
sometimes he forgets not to bite or scratch,

sometimes he forgets he too is a boy.

i hug all my kids before they leave.
the first time i tried to give him a hug,
he thought i was attacking.
it is all he knows about embrace:
it means trapped, caught... and weak
the hair on his back raised and sharp.
          paws ready to defend.
reminded me
being a black boy feels
like you become a mantle piece,
before you become a man.
snared in the world's delusion
of black boys only being animals.

i know this complicated curse,
always having to transform in order to survive
this concrete thicket of death and poverty,
or the moon's prejudice and profiling.
where it's all hunt or be hunted
trying to contain such a necessary beast.
all black boys shapeshift themselves.
to be aggressive,
          growing up in a hood timid could get you
shot.
to be passive,

because showing your teeth to police might
get you shot.

silver bullets come from both the block or a badge.

while the privileged frolic in the prairie
the ability to fail or fight without fear.
no pale gaze making them monsters.

at schools where i've taught
the white kids get mental health
therapy, slap on the wrists.
the black boys get metal detectors
felonies, handcuffs on their wrists.
prison pipelined into muzzle
and collar before they develop a bark.
tried as beasts before seen as humans.
five times more likely to be held in captivity.

i don't want see jeremiah
gripped in a cage
or hanging from a leash.
a boy who just wants to listen
to nursery rhymes
and play football.
i show him love,
because no one has
because he deserves love

and a childhood
because the forest
he's being raised in
is all shadow and predators
and i don't want this madness
to devour another boy.

i show him
my class is sunshine,
never wax nor wane.
crescent or full
new or blue
Nowadays he hugs me
before and after school

he knows he is not an unnatural thing.
he is not folklore.
not a beast. just a boy.
no matter what he sees in the forest.
no matter what the moon says.

dating advice after the death of tamir rice and aiyanna stanley-jones

when you get to the age when i let you date (which if completely left up to me, will not be until your mid-40's). if you decide to date guys, no black guys. we don't always stick around. i imagine that's a little alarming coming from me. don't get me wrong, black men are great father's, loyal lovers, beautiful humans. i'm just scared you'll invest your soul into some man who will soon be blood plastered across a police car. do not bring back a boy who has bullseyes for corneas, *please-don't-shoot* written like an apology between the lines of his palms, whose hands are forced to reach for goals he may not live long enough to achieve. black guys, we all smell like burnt flesh and melting iron, like falsified police reports and altered evidence. me being alive to pass this on is a miracle. do not bring any black guys to this dinner table. this is a dining room. not a morgue.

when you get to the age when i let you date, if you decide to date girls... same rule applies. not because of the stereotypes of being difficult, but of being difficult to find. they shut down an entire city for hannah graham, but alexis patterson was just a whispering headline. black women die just as fast as black men, but they die quietly. the way america wants them too. when the media is dancing around future acquittals of badged men killing sons, they are stepping on the bodies of daughters whose killers never see a courtroom. don't put vanishing images in our family photos. i hold your mother like a seance every night, i don't want you becoming infatuated with a woman that will fade into human trafficking, a forced suicide, stray bullet, or a stack of forgotten statistics on some detective's desk.

if you decide to love a human whose skin is rich, golden, *fatal* as yours. do it. because the roads in your skin will always bring you back to where you came from, will always reflect your own beauty. their eyes will always be two north stars. it's not going to be easy. embrace the war your bodies may endure after a goodbye kiss. some will never know the agony of a battle wound, but never run their fingers across the triumph of a scab. love in the moment, like it's both fleeting and forever. to be black and in love is to love with fervor, and fear, and fight!

but...

if you can't handle a love so dark and brazen. play it
"safe", marry a porcelain cop, pale and fragile, but
more likely to make it back after the *bang*! or a
lover on death row,

at least you'll know when to schedule your tears.

kiss

      on the cheek
      on the forehead.
he's a baby right now,
but when he's 2 i'm going to kiss him
after he pees in the potty all by himself.
at 6, i'm going to kiss his scraped knee
when a bike ride becomes a bull ride.
he'll get a peck atop his head everyday before
school.
at 12, i'm going to hold him when the
first person he puppy loves, dogs him.
when a flood breaks from his eyes,
i will kiss him dry.
17, i'm going to kiss him before prom
and tell him he's gorgeous.
18, a smooch when he graduates.
i'm going to kiss him because
kids are always embarrassed
when their parents kiss them.

i love   embarrassing my children.

i kiss my son because
i kiss my daughter,
but that's not a poem.
fathers are "supposed" to kiss daughters,

"expected" to kiss daughters,
but not sons.

we punch our sons
in the shoulder,
in the chest,
wrestle out the most human
parts of him.
"man up!"
"go hard!"
be a stone.
a wall.
but not like stonewall riot 1969,
because that's *gay*
and fathers are so scared for their sons to be gay.
to be anything different than their assumptions.
we are lied to
and told that gay means sensitive,
sensitive means soft
soft means feminine.
taught that feminine means weak.

fathers are to chisel their sons into gargoyles,
sculptured monsters.
make concrete of their depression
passions,
rejections,
or their sexuality,

make their emotions a fluid,
forgotten center.

i kiss my son,
because my mother could not kiss me,
because my mom was forced to be a dad.
because my dad
was never around
to kiss me,
hold me,
tell me i'm beautiful
or show me that men are more than knuckles and
gravel.
not that he would have anyway,
he comes from a time where manliness is cut from
affection.
patriarchy has always pulled the strings
making men hyper-masculine marionettes
who ball their fists,
grab their nuts,
or attempt to puppeteer women.

masculinity so fragile,
but sculpted by hands that violate and crush .

not my son.
he will not fall into that crater of manhood
where the threat of emasculation

is an earthquake
looming around every shaky compliment.
where even a hug is a tremor,
where "i love you" is a fault line dividing men,
and father's won't embrace their son's cheek
for fear of cracking their face like crust.
the male ego is built like a castle,
but could crumble   with a kiss.

villanelle for the educator

what is there left to do?
i try my best to educate,
but i fear i'll only save a few.

the schools pretend to be their friend, but leave
them without a clue.
so poverty or prison is their fate.
what is there left to do?

it's my opinion, that results are driven, by a child's
hue.
i pull them aside before it's too late,
but i fear i'll only save a few.

time after time, we're told we're prone to crime.
that just isn't true.
for centuries we've continued this debate.
what is there left to do?

my job's to teach. i fear i won't reach but one or
two.
use my influence to fight the incarceration rate,
but i fear i'll only save a few.

because prejudice and ignorance is oppression's witches brew.
in my frustration i ululate
"what is there left to do?!"
[but] i fear i'll only save a few.

august 12th, 2016

my 9 year old and i
are caught in a wave of emotion
watching olympic swimmers.

simone manuel.
first black woman to splash in olympic gold.

before, my daughter thought nothing of swimming
but a goal,
few strokes to check off a bucket list;
a hobby at best.
she now knows this is tangible.
seen a black queen get her crown wet
and wash away the stereotypes of black bodies in
water.

that we do more than sink
and fight the water for not being land.

she can float like butterfly stroke and rage like the
sea.
seeing simone dive into history
showed my baby that black can be ocean and oshun.

the next day,
when the sun is smiling and soaking a motherland

in her skin,
she is in the pool
teaching herself to
be kick
be pull
be thrust
be wave
be current
be brave
be fervent
be breaking records and stigmas

each lap,
a swim across coastlines,
a thank you to simone,
to cullen jones,
to marteiza correia,
to the africans snatched away from the shoreline;
the ones that jumped in the atlantic,
fists still raised on the ocean floor.
and the ones that stayed
and taught us to swim.

a poem about ptsd in three parts
or
to the white guy beaten up by an elderly black man after addressing him as "my nigga" on the subway

i.

when a soldier returns
after watching all his drinking buddies die
poured into the sand as casualties
of america's largest bar brawl called *war*
one he never started and will never finish
scarred flesh
brain still lingering with haunts of
gunshots and screams
the taste of someone else's blood flung on his
bottom lip.
the call for freedom in a bloody stare
when he comes home
everything is still exploding around him
everything becomes a trigger
his reality is nothing like ours
he is always reliving the trauma

ii.

dear john on the subway car,

spare me the colorblind bullshit!

where you dance (off beat) around the history of

that word.

where (you think) rap has given you a pass

to be offensive in sing alongs to favorite hood

anthems.

privately, in the company of wiggers.

and-that-one-token-black-guy-who-let's-you-say-it-

because-

you-both-like-*trap*-music-and-you-let-him-smoke-al

l-the-weed.

dappin' up your "homies" from the cul de sac,

saggin' pants and swag.

everything short of a black face spray tan.

saying "nigga/er" to black millennials may get you

a sassy-ass twitter post and a sarcastic hashtag.

iii.

when a black man who has seen his drinking

buddies die

in america's largest bar brawl called the civil rights

era

a war he didn't start and hasn't seen finished

one that started because he may have been sitting

in the white only section

the scars of riots still evident in flesh
gunshots and screams.
the call for freedom in a bloody stare
and *that* word flung onto his bottom lip
when a black man who has heard "nigga"
in tales from people still clutching freedom papers
like they're going to be repossessed
heard stories of "my nigga" used in possession
[like] last thing heard before leaving an auction
block

when a black man remembers hearing
nigga(er) after *burn*
nigga(er) after *die*
nigga(er) after *get out*
he is always exploding
he is always a trigger
his reality is nothing like yours
he's is reliving the trauma

you wouldn't scream *bang!* in the face of a veteran.
someone who has spent their life dying for mankind
you don't say nigga(er)
                    ever.
especially addressing
someone who has spent his life dying
to prove he is a man.

i don't care who says it

sometimes my black students say nigga. they use it
the way you'd expect them to. the way their parents
use it. in conversation. endearing.

sometimes i get white students who say nigger. they
use it in the way you expect them to. the way their
parents use it. in anger. with malice. aimed
carelessly at the dark.

black students say nigg*a*. with distinction. keeping
"er" in the dark. they know white sheets or snarling
canine is lurking in *"er"*. but oblivious to the
oppression in *their* version.

white students say nigg*er*. even when they say *"a"*.
they say *"er"* with bite. squawk it like crow. racism
broken open in emergencies. spit flying from their
mouth like shattered glass   or fire hoses.

i don't care who says it. they can't say it in my
class. here in virginia, where sixty years ago they
wouldn't have been able to say it in the same room.
where the word birthed riots and legislation. where
it has threaded men to trees. in a space where i
wouldn't have been allowed to teach them. and
these days, english class feels more like history.

breastroke and liberty

flooded with oppression;
survival is a gasp.
necessary breath
for a drowning population.

raised fist:
a lighthouse
in an ocean of faces waiting for change,
leading them to light.

resistance. peaceful or not.
protest and rally are kick and swim.
the wipeout of black bodies
is not a distress call, but call to action.

living is more than treading water.
more side stroke, like lifeguard.
to guard lives
and pull others from sinking.

i will not drown in oppression.
i am both fin and fist.
dolphin kick when others will not,
because ancestors found death and rebirth in the
water.

until my final gasp
i will remain a lighthouse.
a beacon of freedom for those who still swim.
when the law no longer acts as a lifeguard,

but a privileged breath
who will never appreciate change.
preferring minorities as floating bodies
instead of breathing lives.

drowning population.
seeking light.
taking action.
still sinking.

when they tell you the dozen bullets in my chest are suicides

riot!   earthquake.

define disaster.
divine disaster.

be lives lost for a just cause!

be violent against oppression!

be violet blossoming retaliation!

be violins. be unstoppable dissonance!

justice and revenge are the same chords.

pacifism is only appreciated
when they see the destruction that can be done.

so   burn!

until no one can distinguish night from day.

until they cannot distinguish the sun from the fires.

char the white house!

capsize the capitol! let it sink in its capitalism!

be hero for your own,
never destroy your own.
do not destroy the corner store.
nor lay waste to the schools.
not yours.
just   theirs.   them.
force them into ships.
leave their bodies in the ocean.
lay oppressors next   to their victims.

physics lesson for darren wilson

in physics, thermal radiation by objects or bodies

can be measured as blackbody radiation.

the term "blackbody radiation" describes an object that

radiates internally at the same temperature as its environment.

kevlar and steel badge make you more frigid;

you... don't radiate at the same temperature as the bodies

you are sworn to protect.

your temperature, a degree below inhumane,

too low to understand brilliant black bodies in ferguson

or to see that mike was not a black hole in search to consume six more.

blackbody radiation emits light, though it appears black,

as most of the energy cannot be perceived by the human eye.

you, were too "human" to see his

      black body,

human.

all naive adrenaline.

his imperfections outshining his future emanating
inside.

in nature, no blackbody is perfect.

no

       body is perfect.

insulated enclosures contain blackbody radiation

only emitting a light when a hole is made in its wall.

big mike was a large body.

large

       black

           body.

6'4", 300 lbs of energy they never trained you

to harness,

would need way more than one hole in him

to see all the shine within.

why is it our black bodies never seem to stay
enclosed

around

       police?

the bright-blue burning in our bosom

blackened by bright blue flashing lights.

we have been forced to not reflect,

just absorb bullets and beatings.

for centuries, we have been trying to gleam bright
enough for laws

to know we are more than dark unknown boiling to
be incandescent.

we marched with the logic

the more black bodies, the more glow.

boycotted as if taking away our light

would show you how dark this world is without us.

our riots weren't violent, they were ultra-violet.

but here we are still just embers after gunsmoke.

some scientists say blackbody radiation doesn't
exist;

but michael was another star plucked from the
darkness,

and ferguson is more luminous than ever,

blazing bright with piercing protests and bodies so
sick of swallowing abuse

that they've become volcanic.

proof,

that action will always have reaction;

light will always have refraction.

and beware of what you beam at black bodies,

you may not be prepared for what beams back.

ode to the pacifist

death will never die.
murder begets murder
the expansion of rotting flesh
and growing wounds

love is a bloody bandage on intolerance.
it is peace
that works like healing scab
like blood cells bridging a gash.
you cannot destroy destruction.
closed fists
are for force
for cracking skin
tyrannical shot to face
and gives space to be labelled troublemaker.
you can't vilify peace.
it is open hands that holds
structure, balance, communities.
together.
what good is *fight*
if everyone loses.
violence cannot find life.

discover rebirth and redirection
in the heart of peacekeepers.
find passion in the praying palms
and god in the in the other cheek.
it will discover turn.

                    turn are how revolutions begin.

sell fish

bait them in.
keep the the rod and string a trade secret.
hook them into working for what is already theirs
for there is more to gain in feeding a man
than to teach him how to feed himself.

fishers of men, sell fish.
quench his slaving belly
and tell him he has done good
that this fillet is his reward.
promote him and give him more,
2, 3, 4.

for he will take this back to his family
that he is struggling to afford.
his son will grow up with a desire to hunt like his
dad.
grind to skeleton and scale.

because in his eyes his father is a fisherman.
college educated to reach into rivers and wrangle
salmon
in actuality, classrooms have taught him to swim in
schools... like fish.
he settles for this, education costing more than he
may stand to make.

paying to learn, because we are told it pays to learn
in the process, we learn to pay for what need not be
paid for
there was no cost to learn to walk,
the first 13 years of your school career were
practically on the house
then sallie mae/fafsa rents you a net
whatever you catch is your fee
what is left to eat?
why [the fuck] isn't your college education free?

that is the will of god, but it is in cod we trust.
so capitalists sell fish, and say student loans
will get you more. no knowledge of how to cast and
reel in,

fish: a fluid term.
fed to us as a noun
when it's the verb that spawns success
a flood of knowledge might drown the hierarchy
so it's distributed in increments to ensure poverty
exists.

not built to make you independent,
but to trap you in dependence
this is american capitalism
where everything has a fee including what they

teach.

this is the hypocrisy in independence day.

july 4th, 1776, not the beginning where america understood
how to be its own man, but the start when this country learned
how to feed its need for profit by starving its own land.
separating from european control right?
unnecessary tax, big government, wages too low.
just to sail across this fishbowl to america and do the same shit
they hit us with the ol' bait-n-switch.

this country's system of capitalism
is designed to keep you coming back to the lake.
keep at least a quarter of the population hungry,
work to devour your check. and tax half the fish you get.

if you give a man a fish, he will eat and return for more;
willing to do anything for it, but if you teach a man to fish
he will find water, he will build his own pier, teach his peers.
become more verb; more action than consumption.
leaving big business/america/capitalism

a river run dry
from being
           selfish

lady at the counter

i did not think i'd be here.

high school graduate,

three point seven gpa,

mass communications major,

in line

       for tanf.

social services, to me, smelled of failure and

dependence.

not too many men come in here.

       i could tell

       by the way the lady at the counter was

scowling,

as if my gender offended her.

presumed i was using this system like a bank

my daughter,

a blank check.

her expression screamed

"how dare this man come into an institution

designed to assist poor disenfranchised

                                  women

benefits package clasped tighter than dignity.

looser than pride.

enough to wriggle free and hand it

as reluctant as she was to take it.

snatched my application

the way a teacher does a test she catches you

cheating on.

summed me up in seconds

i was a book whose cover looked all too familiar.

taught me how fatal stereotypes could be,

a piece of me died on her desk.

i wanted to defend myself,

but there's no battling with people like her.

had to fight to give me eye contact.

every snide remark, a jab to my

already beaten self-esteem,

she mumbled to me through teeth clenched like a

fist.

"a case worker will be with you, maybe

when we are done assisting these other ladies.

                                        next!"

it seemed like just a few days ago

trials were my only reality.

        me

        a battered soldier on the frontline full of

deadbeats

        with excuses like ammo.

my war took place at a cold desk,

frozen glare from my ex-wife ,

and a judge with a lukewarm compassion for

dedicated dads.

i dodged, icy daggers lunged at my character.

chilling draft

created a biting regret for the tundra i once called a

marriage.

forty-five minutes of frostbite later

i walked away to thaw with my daughter.

full custody is the warmest feeling i have ever

known

but i'm still broke.

a struggling parent

ready to snap at stretching to make ends meet.

and america has deemed only for "babymamas"

now applies to me.
i am somewhat justified,
still very ashamed
to be in this position,
to need such assistance.
on my knees, at the hands
of some bullshit government check until i'm back
on my feet,
[but] proud to be one of the few full time fathers i
know.
willing to sacrifice my stubborn ego by standing in
this line
even if it means enduring condescending remarks
from a woman too busy looking down on me
to understand why my head is held high

never assuming, i was there for my daughter's
first word, first step, first fall,
and i'll be there to catch the rest.
i'll stay for first boyfriend, husband,
first child, and the first time she sacrifices for them,
and i'll be first man in my family to do it.
but you try telling that to
the lady at the counter

not thirst. preparation.

my daughter drinks a lot of water
and i was worried it was because
she's trying to quench the fiery passion in her belly.
[or] so concerned about the singe of failure
she prays to countless bottles of dasani
to drench it.

"my daughter drinks water
like a fish" i'd say in jest,
but i've been looking at it all wrong.
she isn't gills and fins.
she is hydrogen and oxygen.

my daughter drinks water
because she understands this world
will either suffocate you or leave you out to dry,
but nothing evaporates the sea.

my daughter drinks lots of water to replenish.
sometimes her eyes are atlantic and pacific.
even then, there is a continent's worth of resilience
between them.

my daughter drinks a lot of water
and has become a stream of childish innocence,
a tenacity that comes in waves.

her favorite place to be is the beach,
for her it's like looking at a mirror:
she knows when to push people and when to ebb.
she only bows to the moon
and keeps the same crescent smile.

my daughter drinks a lot of water
after every playground session, ballet lesson, fight,
and argument.
the hurricane brewing inside,
        needs all the fuel it can get.

december 27th, 2016

i'm having a conversation with my daughter;
the first part, laughing about how she wanted dress
her brother up in a dress, and second, her feeling
like she must be a boy. we had a long talk about
identity. i asked a lot of questions just to realize this
confusion was sparked by a silly conversation (she
overheard) at school about how "only boys are
supposed to like sports and pokémon" and she likes
all those things. so... she must be a boy.

we talked about gender politics and how
~~she's~~ they're my ~~daughter~~ child and ~~she~~ they can
like whatever ~~she~~ they wants. and identify however
~~she~~ they wants. that's up to ~~her~~ them. i explained all
these things are fluid. *she* determined she's a girl
that likes pokémon and sports. i don't know how
that's going to translate to who she'll be attracted to.
i don't care. the standout moment in our talk was
"daddy, i don't know what i am (awkward laugh)."
and my response, "it doesn't matter. i'll love you
regardless."

the honest part about this, is that this was a little uncomfortable for both of us. there are things i still have to work through as a cis-het man that was raised very "traditional". i'm raising my children to better than me. progress can be uncomfortable. i'm also never going to make my kids feel weird about anything they're feeling. they deserve to be themselves and parents that accept them.

misogyny's guide to womanhood

cook.

>we are designed to hunt you. be sure that once you are captured you know how to prepare yourself to be devoured.

clean.

>sweep, dust, scrub anything that we feel is unpleasant. your flaws are dirty. we keep things messy enough.

fuck.

>when you want to. when you don't. this is your main responsibility.

fuck.

>know how to speak when you do it. know when to say it is ours. it is always ours.

fuck.

>remember adverbs are for men. we are the only ones allowed to fuck *up*, *over*, or *around*.

fold.

>nothing is sexier than a woman who is willing to bend for us.

tuck.

      draw together all signs of human: stretch
marks, cellulite, opinions, and expectations.

your body can do more.
will be demanded more.
but supply and demand
work differently
with a frugal male ego.
your worth will drop
the less you adhere
to the price of submission.

barefeet

when you grow up as poor as i did, designer high tops were a luxury my mother couldn't afford. in this fashion show called a basketball court, i didn't make the cut. a mockery of the sport. so in pickup games, i sat sideline while piercing pointer fingers seared holes into my payless sneakers. it felt like jordan was laughing at me personally,

the more i came to play, the more ridicule ensued the playground. claimed my bargain brands wouldn't make it. so one day i took them off; exclaimed i could beat all of them barefoot. toe to toe with my haters. no socks. they let me play to make me to the laughing stock of the blacktop. i played to prove that shoes don't make the baller; real ballers just make plays.

i barely won that game. nearly lost toenails in the process. heels deflated and punished by my own pride. too proud to notice the agonizing pain. crowned in shocked expressions. i regretted it then, but it toughened my skin for the long walk ahead of me.
kids can be cruel, like life, like failure. rejection did not stop at the basketball court and bullies don't stop after school.

in this game of life we are all players.

the hall of fame is for soles who stand strong and
play hard. triumph is formed by running, uphill,
past oppression, tennis-shoes pad you from reality.
my feet didn't get bruised in that game, they got
prepared; they got armored for the people willing to
step on your toes to stay a step ahead keep your
brand names: jordan's, and lebron's. nike can't go
hard in the paint when i've laced up my
determination.

you don't know what it truly means to win
until you have walked a mile in my calluses.

to darling nikki

we listened in guilty pleasure
at tales of your taboo debauchery
not understanding
that you were a queen
who took your subjects
to your castle,
let them bow at your crown,
lift your gown,
draped thighs over shoulders
and knighted   us

the names they called you (d)evolved
jezebel
harlot
slut
thot

but you changed for no man

taking what you desired
leaving like thief from the knight
the way they left so many women before you.
and in the sheets of their mulish pride
you can hear them moan
come back nikki!
come back!

dearly beloved, an ode

strophe

"*dearly beloved,*
we are gathered here today
to get through this thing called
 life"

electric word life
sang a livewire i adored, who wore taller heels and
more makeup,
than my mother on easter or a club night.
a sinners hymnal of the
unapologetic-sexy-sinner-saint
blasphemed and baptized
an altar call of baritone whine
a mix between louisiana-brimstone pastor and
unending orgasm.
anomalous androgynous prophet
praise like it's 1999
saved us from thieves
we dance in the strobe-light temple
amen, amen, and amen

antistrophe

for the same brand of men who raised me
kneeled before this royal's flare, swag, and '81
cm400
for men crying violet tears for prince,
but hold violence for *queens*
for the men who paint their son's blue-black
when they are too purple
for men who only tolerate a man wearing heels,
when he makes music you can fuck to.
for the men who learned next-to-nothing from the
music, but the sex
and only for their gain
repent, repent, repent

epode

fluid as the rain filling lakes where souls are
purified
blended to show the balance we are.
embodiment of a sign indistinguishable and fluid
lovechild of venus and mars
we all lost ourselves in this conduit of uncensored
art
an electric word,
no matter what bias and bigotry lined the lips of
those who kiss
they thanked the weeping bird,

and seeing god in the most godless gospel of places
it is not a woman, it is not a man
hallelujah to the miracles
of something that we will never understand
to never letting the elevator take us down
to april snow
and for the souls captured in the pressure of societal
norms
emerging from below:

a diamond
a pearl
a hallelujah, hallelujah,
hallelujah

choosing the chrysalis

moths and butterflies both emerge from cocoons.
the beauty inside the chrysalis is based upon
perception.
once hatched, they both fly toward the sun.
one paints its wings in the light, one chooses to
burn.

the beauty of the human experience is the
opportunity of rebirth.
the moth, without thought, is engulfed by it's bad
decisions.
humans look within before they set their self ablaze.
however, humans look at their self and fear what
they see.

i began moving forward when i stopped looking in
the mirror.
the mirror shows you who you are already.
i replaced all my mirrors with paint and canvas.
i want to create who i am choosing to be.

i am the perfect mistake.
mistakes are the only things human do perfectly.
perfection is not the absence of flaws in existence.
perfection is the acceptance all things in existence
are flawed.

the human experience is a cocoon.
the beauty in this experience is the opportunity of
rebirth
but when i look in the mirror
i struggle not seeing a mistake.

my chrysalis is based upon my perception.
i can either be engulfed by my bad decisions,
and be nothing better that what i am already,
since mistakes are the only things humans do
perfectly.

or, when i fly towards the sun,
i can look within before i set myself ablaze.
i am the framework of my canvas.
i am a perfectly flawed existence,

one that paints its wings with fire, and does not
burn.
i no longer look at the mirror and fear what i see.
my vision now shows what i am choosing to be.
i am perfect because i have accepted that i am
flawed.

About the Author

Douglas Powell/Roscoe Burnems is a longtime spoken-word artist and poet, National Poetry Slam champion (2014), 3rd place regional finalists (2009, 2014), and former coach of Good Clear Sound (VCU's poetry slam team ranked 3rd internationally 2018). Born and raised in Richmond, VA Douglas/Roscoe also works a community organizer, educator, mentor, in addition to be a loving husband, and dedicated father of two.

Facebook: Roscoe Burnems
IG: @thewritersdenrva
www.roscoeb.webs.com
www.thewritersdenrva.com

Made in the USA
Middletown, DE
12 July 2023

34745976R00040